# HOW TO PAINT
## *Flames*

Pat Kytola & Larry Kytola

Motorbooks International
Publishers & Wholesalers

We would like to dedicate this book to all the people who in the past, present and future have had a hand in the start and preservation of custom painting.

A special thanks to the following: Tex Smith for historical pictures; Gene Winfield for the historical facts; and Herb Martinez for all the phone calls, time, historical facts and encouragement.

A large thank you also goes to Timothy Remus who shot the how-to sequence on custom painting and David H. Jacobs, Jr., for the use of his product and equipment photographs.

Finally, a thanks to all the people who have allowed me to capture their cars on film for inclusion in this book. The interest in and the love of the American automobile continues to grow, and painting flames on them is as unique today as it was in the beginning.

**On the front cover:** *The custom 1955 Oldsmobile Holiday Coupe owned by Sonny and Lisa Rogers of Independence, Missouri. The black base coat is acrylic enamel. The flames started with a brilliant yellow base with red fogged over and blue flame tips added. A Sherwin Williams clear coat was sprayed over the flames with a clear top coat flaked with finely ground gold mica. Timothy Remus*

**On the back cover:** *How to paint flames with step-by-step photos in color and black and white following one project from start to finish.*

**On the frontispiece:** *Many street rodders have a soft spot in their heart for a Ford Model A—especially with flames! Barry Bowers of York, Pennsylvania, owns this 1930 A painted blue with red flames. The paint work was done by J's Custom paint studio.*

**On the contents page:** *An Auto Scooter bumper car that has also received a set of flames. The bumper car has been converted into a trailer and painted yellow. A set of flames was then applied using orange, blue and red paint. The flames were outline-stripped using a wide white strip. Leave it to rodders to modify and customize just about anything that moves!*

First published in 1990 by Motorbooks International Publishers & Wholesalers, P O Box 2, 729 Prospect Avenue, Osceola, WI 54020 USA

Motorbooks International is a certified trademark, registered with the United States Patent Office

The information in this book is true and complete to the best of our knowledge. All recommendations are made without any guarantee on the part of the author or publisher, who also disclaim any liability incurred in connection with the use of this data or specific details

We recognize that some words, model names and designations, for example, mentioned herein are the property of the trademark holder. We use them for identification purposes only. This is not an official publication

Motorbooks International books are also available at discounts in bulk quantity for industrial or sales-promotional use. For details write to Special Sales Manager at the Publisher's address

Library of Congress Cataloging-in-Publication Data
Kytola, Pat.
    How to paint flames / Pat Kytola and Larry Kytola.
       p.  cm.
    ISBN 0-87938-421-2
    1. Automobiles—Decoration.  2. Automobiles—Customizing.  I. Kytola, Larry.  II. Title.
TL154.K97 1990
629.26—dc20                        90-5662
                                   CIP

Printed and bound in Hong Kong

# Contents

# *Flames*

# Flames: The Legends

Flames on hot rods are part of what makes hot rods hot. The traditional flames of the early hot rodding days were flagrant bursts of fire burning bright from around the rod's front grille, flowing across the hood and over the tops of the fenders. The colors were a sunburst of brilliant red, orange and yellow, often outlined with white pinstriping. Later, flames became more flowing, with long tongues of fire stretching all the way to the front doors—and beyond! In the 1990s, a new fire was sparked in hot rod paintwork. The traditional flames gave way to modern high-tech computerized flame graphics, swirls of pinstriped flame designs, subdued pastel hues, neon colors—and a renewal of the old-fashioned scallops and other styles of custom painting. Through it all, the tradition of hot rodding flames has burned bright.

Yet while most hot rodders agree on the cool of flames and custom painting, few agree on where the idea of painting flames on a hot rod began. Legends, tall tales, shadetree-painters' lore, hot rod bench-racing myths—there are probably as many true stories of who painted the

first flames as there are hot rods and hot rodders. Sometimes our pioneering hero used plain old paintbrushes, sometimes a spray gun, and sometimes the car was parked in the backyard and a vacuum cleaner filled with paint was set on reverse and used as an air gun. In fact, the only truth worth betting on is that the abundance of history is part of the fun. Here are several of the best stories from some of the best storytellers.

**Legend.** LeRoi "Tex" Smith, everyone's favorite publisher of *Hotrod Mechanix* magazine, recalls it this way, telling the story in his inimitable drawl.

The forerunners of flames were the swooping scallop designs painted on the hot rod pioneer airplane racers that soared around the pylons in the early 1930s glory days of air racing in the United States. The flyboys painted long sweeping scallops along the front edges of the airplanes' wings and around the engine cowling on the nose. The scallops were a natural fit inbetween bulges on the cowling, which was shrunk as small as possible for streamlining; the bulges were necessary to clear the rocker covers on the engines. These scallops were often in bright colors to identify and glorify the racing planes, and outlined with pinstripes to define the lines. Some of the famed racers, such as the muscle plane Gee Bees and the Wedell-Williamses, were emblazoned with brilliant scallops from nose to tail, wing tip to wing tip.

*Traditional hot licks on a 1940 Ford hailing from Texas. The car's base color is a bright medium blue, setting off the flames well. The fire starts as white at the nose, blending to yellow, orange and finally red at the tips of the flames.*

Later in the 1930s, the speedway and dirt-track car racers picked up on the airplane jockeys' idea. Scallops ran the length of these heyday racers, such as the Gilmore Oil Company Speedway Special and other outlaw sprint dirt-trackers. Yet it wasn't until an early issue of *Hot Rod* magazine ran a photograph on its cover of a guy named Bob McCoy with his 1940 Ford festooned in flames that the trend caught on.

***Legend.*** Another, unattributed story states that the idea for fancy paint work came not from the air racers but from the air fighters and bombers of World War II. The P-38 Lightning and P-51 Mustang fighters often were painted with huge shark's teeth mouths under their engines to strike fear into the hearts of German and Japanese adversaries. Bombers like the B-17 Flying Fortresses and the B-25 Mitchells wore warpaint nose art, with accompanying smart-aleck logos, copying the Vargas poster girls, Walt Disney characters and other popular culture of the period.

Returning home after the war to their gals and their old jalopies in Smalltown, USA, the boys had time on their hands and the beautiful artwork of the airplanes on their minds. The warpaint artwork became the model for flames as a way to beautify their mundane prewar cars.

***Legend.*** Historian Don Montgomery, author of several photographic collections evoking the early hot rodding days, remembers it differently. Flames originated in the form of scallops with the early car customizers who were seeking radical new ways to highlight the lines on their cars. Hot rodders of the era, meanwhile, were primarily cutting down their cars and concentrating on souping up the engine and driveline to beat out the next guy at the Saturday night stoplight drags. The custom car shows of the 1950s put the spotlight on bodywork, and custom painting emphasized the designs. Hot rodders hit on the scallops second, as Montgomery remembers it.

***Legend.*** On the warm night of October 20, 1938, the midget racers were tearing up the track at the infamous Gilmore Speedway in Hollywood, California, as they had many nights before. Blasting along the track, a driver named Fred

*Cars don't have the corner on trick flame jobs. Chuck Haas of Tewsbury, Massachusetts, drove his flamed 1936 pickup from the East Coast of the United States to Minnesota during the summer of 1989 for the Nationals. Some body styles sport flames better than others, and the traditional black vehicle with the addition of yellow, orange and red flames will always remain popular.*

According to LeRoi "Tex" Smith, hot rodders got the idea of flames via the daring airplane racers of the early 1930s. This Gee Bee racer was a true muscle plane—all engine, with a squat little body and short, fat wings. The long swooping scallops on the body-work and the wheel covers were the spark to ignite the idea of flames. This airplane also boasts some fancy nose art with the lucky seven and eleven painted on the front.

Another hot rodding legend attributes the inspiration for flames to the fighter airplanes of World War II, which often had bold paint schemes to strike fear into the adversaries. This one wears a dramatic shark's mouth under its nose and along the cowling. In the photo, the plane looks about to eat its pilot.

Friday crashed his midget, which burst into a spectacular fire. A track photographer swung his handy press camera towards the scene and caught the instant in a great shot of the flaming sprinter. The hapless Fred Friday wasn't terribly lucky that night but his burning car became the inspiration for painting flames on hot rods.

**Legend.** Australian hot rodding journalist David Fetherston, while doing research on a book chronicling the heroes of hot rodding, has discovered what he thinks is the earliest known set of flames. The year was 1948, just after World War II. Fourteen-year-old Joe Bailon from the San Francisco Bay area, who would later go on to become a famous customizer, had a hot rod that

*Hot rodding history began with the track roadsters of the early 1940s and 1950s. Here is the Gilmore Speedway Special racer, complete with scallop paintwork running back from the grille. The scallops are simple and basic, without any sort of pinstriping to highlight them. The lion painted on the body could have come from the World War II bomber nose art, as some suspect. The driver and his admirers here certainly look proud.*

was as far from hot as the planet Pluto was from the sun. Under the four-piece hood of the 1929 Ford Model A Coupe sat an embarrassing stock four-cylinder engine with about as much guts and horsepower as a cement block.

Using two paint brushes—"a big one and a little one," Fetherston says—and a couple cans of different colored paint, Bailon drew flames emitting from the louvers on the side of the hood. What Bailon did to the car has been a hot rodder's trick for forever and a day. He painted the car so at least it looked hot—and suddenly it was hot!

The Bonneville Salt Flats played a large part in hot rodding lore—where else could you actually drive your rod to its limits? As this photograph shows, the Flats also played a role in the development of flames. This record car was made out of a fuel tank used by airplane bombers in World War II, a popular and simple way to build aerodynamic bodywork at the time. The flames here are bold and dramatic, running the whole length of the car. Tex Smith

Midget racer "Cyclone" Ross carried the checkered flag after he won this heat race in Chicago in the early 1930s or 1940s. Ross had come a long way with his paint scheme since the scallops of the Gilmore Special. These flames are crude, and appear more similar to an actual fire than the cartoon-like version of flames that became popular later on. Tex Smith

Back to basics. Driver Grant Lambert's number 44 racer has been painted in two colors with the scallops providing the drama. The race here was at the Firestone Boulevard Motordrome. Tex Smith

A set of flames on an early track roadster. The major development here is the use of a darker colored pinstripe to outline and highlight the flames. This pinstriping certainly set off the flames and distinguished them from the bodywork. Tex Smith

"Joltin'" Johnny Mantz at the wheel of the Agajanian Special in the early 1950s. The car wore a basic set of flames coming off of the nose and also emitting from behind the driver—one of the earliest photos of flames on a car somewhere beyond just the hood! A similar Agajanian Special won the 1952 Indianapolis 500 at the hands of driver Troy Ruttman. Tex Smith

**Legend.** Master custom painter Dave Bell of St. Paul, Minnesota, recalls the first flamed cars he ever saw as being in the pages of the 1950s car magazines. One car that stuck in his mind was from a 1958 *True Men's* pulp magazine. The artist was Von Dutch, who had been painting flames on just about anything that moved, from race cars to motorcycle gas tanks, beginning in the late 1940s. The magazine subject was a Mercedes-Benz 300SL Gullwing, one of the most luxurious sports cars of the era. Von Dutch had been up all night laying out the flames and painting by the numbers. The result? "A mind-snapping paint job that caused accidents on the street," Bell says.

Other early flame jobs Bell remembers in-cluded the T-Bucket roadster built by Norm Grabowski for the TV show, *77 Sunset Strip.* The car was dressed in 1956 Dodge Blue, set off by flames created by Dean Jeffries.

Bell laid his first set of flames in 1958, work-ing his magic with a spray gun on a 1949 Ford stock car racer. The flames, of course, were red.

So, take your pick. There are certainly enough stories to go around—and more than enough tellers.

When it comes down to it, all the stories are probably true. The influences that inspired hot rodders in different parts of the country added up over the years following World War II, and the result was the hot rodder's flames.

In the traditional style—or is it? The flames are simple, bold and pure, and truly highlight the rod. The license plate says "Krooze," and that's just what this fenderless 1934 Ford Roadster does best. The bright yellow base coat with the fuchsia flames are pinstriped with blue. Note that the flames even run onto the frame! The running boards and bumpers have been eliminated.

Flames make it to the street in the 1960s aboard this Chevrolet coupe. The flames are subtle in color combination and have no pinstriped outline, yet the design of fire is wild and sinewy. Tex Smith

Next page

A fresh approach to flames need not be the high-tech approach. The styling of the flames is based on the traditional style, but the long expanse of fire running from the grille all the way around the rear end is certainly novel and dramatic. This street rod, a 1933 Ford three-window coupe, has a lengthened front end, built to look like the early track-style hot rods. The black body is an excellent background for this inferno of flames ranging in color from red to orange to yellow. The orange wheels accent the car nicely.

15

# *Flames*

# Styles of Flames

The hall of fame of hot rodding is full of great painters, and most of them have tried their hand at flames at some time. Many of these hot rodding heroes have become household names: Gene Winfield, Joe Bailon, Von Dutch, Larry Watson, Tommy the Greek, Ed "Big Daddy" Roth, Don "The Egyptian" Boeke, Mike DeWhite, Joe Bailon, Mike Haase, Art Himsh, Rod Powell, Billy the Kid, Mark "The Wizard" Fenyo, Dave Bell, Dean Jeffries, the A Brothers, Joe Anderson. The list goes on and on.

## Spray-gun magicians

Gene Winfield started Windy's Custom Shop in 1947. In 1955, he moved his business to Modesto, California, and the name was changed to Winfield's Custom Shop. Winfield's customers could get chopped tops, channeled and sectioned bodies, fade-away fenders, Frenched lights, custom-made grilles, hubcaps, dash panels, and filled fender and body seams—not to mention the best in custom painting.

Winfield perfected the technique of blending paint colors along the side of a car body, running from light to dark shades of one color or even blending from one color to another. A fine example of Winfield's work is *Jade Idol*, a customized 1956 Mercury. Winfield's latest customizing feat is the construction of fiberglass 1941–48 Fords with chopped tops and molded-in fenders and hoods.

Joe Bailon has an arm-long resume in the custom paint field. Among his credits is the invention of Candy Apple Red paint, which in turn led to other Candy Apple colors. Bailon is well-known for his mixing of colors that are then applied to the car body with a mirror finish. He is also famous for his custom bodywork and styling.

Von Dutch was born as Kenny Howard but became a legend under his nickname. He was the first hot rod pinstriper, and his striping was unlike anything that preceded it. Most of his work hinted at faces or other features, and it is said that he would stripe your car strictly from the vibes he received from you when you first

*Here are two of nature's primary colors but in hues rarely seen in the great outdoors—and who would have thought of flames mingling the two? Using these bright greens and yellows, Dave Koval of Champion, Michigan, applied yet another angle to the flames on his 1939 Ford. Most of the time the painter chooses to start on the front of the car with the color of the flames; Dave chose to start out with the base color. He then applied the flames on top of that, finishing up again with the base color. A nice twist to the norm. Other features on Dave's car that add to the pizzazz are the painted custom headlight rims that replace the standard chrome ones, dechromed hood, lack of a bumper and filled bumper slots. The grille is from a 1940 Deluxe Ford. Overall, the look is smooth.*

A fine example of what good planning can do! John and Sue Swick of Dayton, Indiana, used flames upon flames on their 1940 Ford. Take a long admiring look at the rainbow of colors used: red, blue, yellow, gold, pink and so on. What a collection! Another detail: the outside flames are pinstriped, the inside ones are not. Also note that part of the grille is painted gold. This, along with the chromework, adds the finishing touch to this unique Ford.

met. Von Dutch was one of the first to paint flames on hot rods in the 1940s. One of his secrets was using scrolls in custom painting to nicely hide the round grinder marks. He is also credited with being one of the first to do airbrush art on T-shirts.

We have Larry Watson, also of California, to thank for the long, sinewy, flowing type of flames that are still hot today. He may have been taught custom painting tricks by Von Dutch, but he's become famous in his own right.

Never to be forgotten in the custom painting field is Ed "Big Daddy" Roth, known for his talent in custom lettering and pinstriping. Roth is one of the finest stripers in the field. He got his start in the late 1950s by running ads in the small car magazines where he and his partner "The Baron" advertised striping brushes, paint, decals and weird shirts.

A deviation from tradition on this hot 1934 Ford. The paintwork utilizes the traditional flame colors, but not the traditional design. This car is owned by Suzy and Fred Focchi of Highland Park, Illinois. The fat flames compliment the body design so gracefully that if they were not there this three-window coupe would not be the crowd stopper that it is.

This 1929 Ford Tudor wears a relatively traditional set of flames but the color scheme is radical! The flames start out red blending to purple, blue and bright pink. Note the wide pinstriping in bright pink. Pinstriping is the final step in outlining the flames and takes care of the rough edges, giving the flames a finished look. Pinstriping flames is also easier to do than most pinstriping—you have a pattern to follow!

Tommy the Greek hailed from the San Francisco Bay area. He came from a family of sign painters and got his start in custom painting by striping fire engines back in the 1950s.

## Other custom painting styles

Flames are without a doubt the most famous form of hot rod custom painting, but there have been numerous other truly wild paint styles tried over the years.

One such idea was Stardust painting, a radical finish developed by Tony Bruskivage of the North Jersey Custom Shop. In 1961 the Stardust metal-flake pigment sold for $8 a pound and it took approximately three pounds to finish an average size car. You had a choice of the fine- or coarse-grain Stardust. The procedure was similar to other paint jobs but the outcome was quite different.

First, the original finish was sanded and the area completely cleaned. The car was primed, then sanded, making sure the area was clean and smooth. Next a few coats of color were applied. The Stardust pigment was then mixed with the proper amount of clear lacquer and, using 40 to 50 pounds of air pressure, the lacquer and Stardust pigment were sprayed onto the body panels. Several coats of clear lacquer were applied over the Stardust finish. The finish was sanded with 80 grit sandpaper and more clear coats applied. Finally the finish was color-sanded with fine sandpaper and rubbed out with compound. The car was then ready to show.

Similar to Stardust was glitter painting—applied in basically the same manner, except a gold powder underbase was used before spraying clear lacquer. The glitter was mixed in the spray gun using a 2:1 ratio of glitter and clear lacquer. Adding nuts and bolts to the reservoir for agitation, the mixture was sprayed on. The gun pot needed to be shook constantly to keep the glitter mixed.

*A further step forward in two-toning. This is a high-tech modern set of flames that the hot rodders of the 1950s probably never imagined they'd see. An iron black base coat is adorned with bright fuchsia pink flames to cover this 1940 Chevrolet two-door sedan owned by Thom and Judy Norman of Burbank, Illinois. The three-inch top chop, Frenched stock headlights, 1953 Oldsmobile taillights and the flames make this Chevy stand out.*

Glitter-Flitter hubcaps were another of the custom ideas that had their heyday. Sparkle could be purchased from the local art store. The design was laid out on a hub cap, measured off and masked. Glue was applied thoroughly to the area you wanted covered and then rubbed on with your finger. The glitter powder was then spread liberally over the wet glue. After the glitter was set, the excess was shook off, and you were ready to blast down to the local drive-in and show off your set of Glitter-Flitter hubcaps.

Chrome tape was a hot custom trend as well. The 3M company made a fine polyester pressure-sensitive tape that worked well for the budget hot rodder. The area to be striped was measured out and a strip of masking tape was applied for the border. A strip of chrome tape was laid down followed by another masking tape border for perfect placement of the chrome tape. You had to smooth the chrome tape carefully; if an air bubble could not be smoothed out, it was carefully pricked with a knife or pin, then smoothed out with fingertip or cloth. Masking tape was again added at the bottom edge of the chrome tape to

*Next page*

*A modern color scheme for an old rod. Developing on the original flames, rodders have simplified the color schemes to a two-tone design. But this two-toning is nothing like the Ford or Chevrolet factory paintwork! Yellow and pink are colors that you don't often see together but this is one good-looking ride. Mike and Debbie Lynch of Northlake, Illinois, choose Chicago Street Rods, Chicago, Illinois, to paint their 1938 Ford Deluxe Tudor Sedan yellow with Panther Pink flames. Adding to the neat look on the exterior of the Lynch car is the five-inch top chop; shaved rain gutters; the lack of door handles and trim, smoothed running boards; sunken license plate; and filled cowl vent, grille and crank holes.*

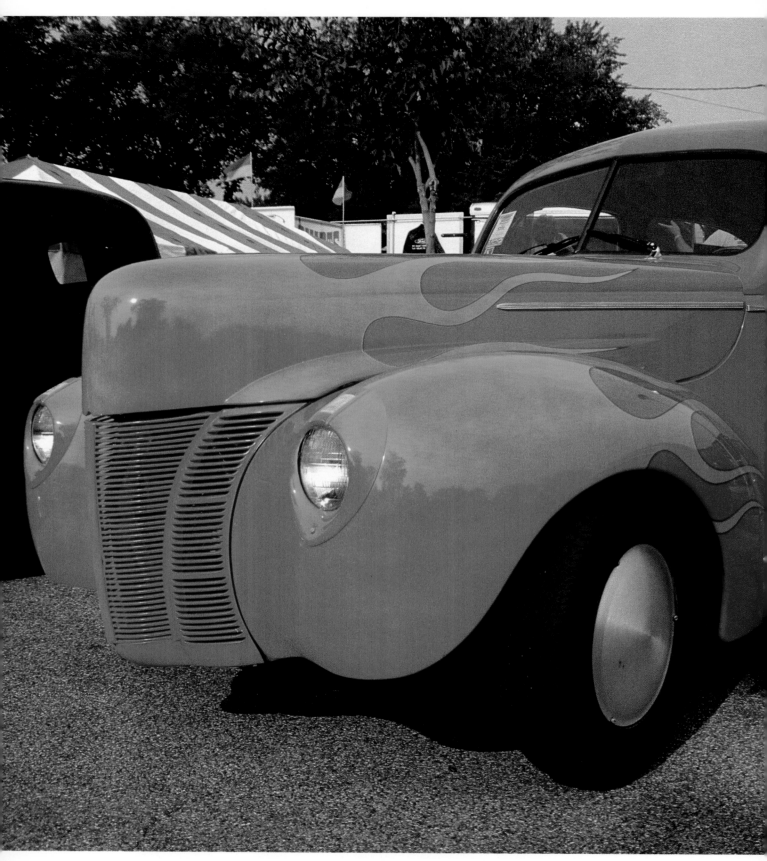

*Pink and red! Hard to believe! In years past when styles and colors were more traditional the combination of these two colors would have been frowned on even by hot rodders. No longer. This 1940 Ford Tudor Sedan owned by Garry White of Marshalltown, Iowa, wears one of the nicest sets of flames around. The colors contrast just right—it's even possible not to notice the flames if you aren't looking closely. Talk about a street sleeper!*

even up bottom edges of tape—accuracy was the byword!

An Exacto knife or razor blade was used, following the edge of the masking tape, to cut the chrome tape evenly to make the edge. After the area was covered with tape and cut evenly, the masking tape was removed and the entire area sprayed with a coat or two of clear lacquer for a final gloss.

Eerie-Dess was named for the eerie design it created. The key ingredient here was household plastic wrap. You would spray on a liberal coat of paint where you wanted this effect, then lay the wrinkled plastic wrap directly on top of the wet paint. When you pulled off the wrap, it left a marble mosaic pattern.

For a variation on the eeriness, you could use aluminum foil or a sponge. After the paint was dry, a coat of clear was added. The effect was strange—a sure hit at the meets.

Cobwebbing was another trick paint idea. To perform the spider's work, you applied lacquer paint without thinning it first. It flowed from the gun and scattered over the surface in threadlike cobweb patterns. This method created high and low spots so several layers of clear paint had to be applied to make the surface even.

Acetylene painting has also been used for custom jobs. After applying your color or a base-coat for candy paints, you sparked your welding torch and, using acetylene only without oxygen,

*Next page*

*An interesting variation on the theme. Ken Kroschel of Berthoud, Colorado, wanted something out of the ordinary painted on his 1939 Chevrolet Sedan Delivery. He and Scott Koehler of Longmont, Colorado, came up with this amazing set of flames blending a 1950s design with modern color schemes. All in all, it required 54 plus hours and over 3,000 feet of ⅛ inch masking tape just to lay out the flames. The work was well worth it. The base coat covered with a substantial clear coat actually changes color depending on the lighting conditions. The flames are painted Chevy white, pearl green and red.*

Here's another color combination that would have gotten the painter kicked out of a 1950s custom show. Hailing from Palos Park, Illinois, Patrick M. Huels owns this 1937 Chevrolet two-door sedan. Traditionally, pink was the color for baby girls, blue for baby boys. This flame job combines the two into a modern look, and in fact, pink and blue are becoming popular colors in all areas of automotive customizing from rods to sport trucks. The painter also altered the traditional flame job placement on this car, moving the fire further back, almost to the windshield, and then flowing down over the running boards!

moved the torch over the surface laying on the smoke to get the desired effect.

Fish scaling, card masking, lace painting, freak drops, graphic stenciling, spaghetti striping, gold leaf paneling, wood graining and numerous mediums have been tried over the years, but flaming has always had a stronghold on hot rodders.

A craze tried by the amateurs who could not afford to have their cars flamed and striped was paper taping, using stick-um 12-inch wide masking paper from your local sign, art or paint shop. The surface to be painted was first cleaned with a grease and wax remover. You then laid the stick-um paper in place, drawing the design directly on the paper with a soft pencil. With a razor blade or sharp knife, you then cut away the design that you had drawn. It was important to do a good job of cutting because the next step, removing the paper, depended on your cutting skill. After the edges of your paper pattern were touched up, steel wool was used to smooth the surface, and more paper was added around the edge to catch the overspray.

Using a small spray gun and low air pressure, you would then fog on your color, using

A tasteful rendering of the traditional flames using a stylish color combination. Al and Sandy Henderson and their 1940 Ford Standard coupe reside in Green Rock, Illinois. The coupe is painted red with metallic gold front end flames that flow back all the way over the doors. Note how the gold changes color until it is almost blue at the tips—a trick of the blue pinstriping. This Ford also has smoothie running boards, painted wheels with beauty rings and hubcaps. All the emblems and chrome are still intact.

lacquer to keep colors evenly fogged. After the lacquer had dried for at least two days, the surface could be rubbed out and the outline of the flame striped.

Some of the flames shown here are traditional in design; some use more scrolling and swirling, offshoots of the fire flame patterns. There will always be some customizers that prefer flames over all the other forms of custom paint—and it's hard to blame them!

Red, white and blue flames—and two sets! The owner of this Ford F-100 pickup must have felt that if one set of flames were good, two would be twice as good. The base color of the truck is white, with the front set of flames blue and the second set of flames red. There is no pinstriping on the edges, nor did he use candy colors.

*An interesting set of flames based on differing hues of green. The medium green flames complement the lighter green body color, and the bright yellow pinstriping* *sets off the two quite well. This 1947 Ford is owned by Randy Wegner of Plymouth, Wisconsin.*

*Next page*

*Streamer flames of white, pink and yellow on an orange 1936 Ford Tudor Sedan. Quite a wild color scheme! The car also boasts several other modifications, especially the convertible conversion work. The detail work also showcases the hot rodding style of the 1980s. Some rodders like classy chromework on their cars; others prefer to remove it for a streamlined look. One of the latest trends is to apply paint to cover the chrome pieces. On this Ford the door handles, horn covers and wheel rims have all been painted. In terms of final appearance, the painted chrome downplays the trim and highlights the flames. Something to consider! Spun aluminum disks add to the appearance of the car.*

A unique combination of flames upon flames. There are three sets of flames gracing this 1948 Chevrolet Sedan Delivery owned by Dale and Ruth Peeler of Denver, Colorado. The first set is dark orange and shows up only in spots under the heavier red set of flames. A "shadow" set of flames made up from different colors of pinstriping follows the form of the other two sets. Amazing! The white body color shows off the flames well.

The streamer flames used long, sinewy tendrils stretching along the whole length of the car's bodywork, an interesting offshoot of the traditional flames styling. This 1951 lime green Mercury is adorned with gold metalflake streamer flames. The custom also sports a DeSoto grille and Plymouth bumpers. The headlights have been Frenched and Dodge Lancer hubcaps added. The Lakes pipes add to the look as does the tunneled radio antenna, the chopped top and the lack of door handles.

# *Flames*

# How to Paint Flames: Planning

Steve Hendrickson, longtime hot rod buff and editor of *Rodder's Digest*, remembers seeing the photograph of Bob McCoy and his 1940 Ford on the cover of an issue of *Hot Rod* magazine in 1957. At the time, the car's flame paintwork was stunning, a spark that ignited the growing custom painters and fanned the fires of early hot rodding. As Hendrickson recalls, "It was the first really popular flame job and it got a lot of attention."

The beauty of those flames was not only in their novelty. The flames were also sharp in their own right, a splendid blend of colors that set off the car's styling. Around the grille, the flames began white hot, burst into glorious yellow and then brilliant red at their tips. The paint had been sprayed on and color-sanded to achieve the blending effect. All in all, the paint job was a success that brought popularity to a fashion.

Trick paint can do more to spiff up a car than any other single modification. There are no rules; the only guidelines are your own creativity, imagination and ability—just as it was with the first hot rodders. Simplicity may be the key, as with Bob McCoy's pioneering flames. Or, you may opt for the ultimate in high-tech graphics. The choice is up to you.

## Planning your flames: The fun begins

All sets of flames are not created equal. There are beautiful flames, ugly flames and those in-between that are unexceptional and downright uninspiring.

In general, you want your flames to look alive, like a real fire burning. Catching the motion of a real fire in a static, one-dimensional display is where the art comes in. As a rule, the flames work best if they are long and sinewy; they need to flow and be curvaceous to capture the idea of the burning fire.

There are several tricks that help make flames come alive. The first involves overlapping the flames—running the threads of the fire across each other, or even interweaving. This requires foresight in planning your flames and a deft hand

*Tom McMullen has been long associated with the hot rodding hobby. Based in Anaheim, California, Tom has built some exceptional cars, such as this 1932 Ford Tudor Sedan which he later converted into a Phaeton. Pay special attention to the flames: there are actually several layers of flame paintwork. The front set is orange fading into white and yellow; the second set is white and yellow going into red and blue. Finally, the flames are outlined in white pinstriping. Such beautiful work requires extensive planning and preparation but is possible if you do the job right from the start. Professional results are possible if you think, plan and calculate like a pro.*

The choice of colors for your flames is probably the most important decision you will make when laying out a set of flames—even more important than the actual flame design. The color scheme can either accentuate the flames, hide them or ruin them. Pay close attention to contrasting colors and complimentary colors before you begin the actual paintwork. You must also consider the base color of the car's bodywork and the color of your pinstriping to outline the flames, if you are going to stripe them. Most paint manufacturers have color charts that they distribute to their dealers. These charts offer a wealth of information for comparing color schemes. David H. Jacobs, Jr.

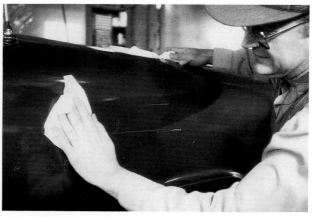

The next step in any painting procedure is a thorough cleaning with a wax and grease remover to rid the bodywork of any road tar, oil, grease or traces of silicone wax. Failure to clean the car can cause problems with the final paint finish, such as fish eyes or poor adhesion. Most paint manufacturers sell their own wax and grease remover products; Ditzler's DX-330 Acryiclean works well. Follow the manufacturer's instructions as some of these products can attack the car's finish if not used properly. Working a small area, clean the entire surface to be painted. Saturate a clean cloth with the wax and grease remover, then wet down a small area. While the surface is still wet, dry it carefully with a clean dry cotton cloth.

The first step in preparing a car for a flame paint job or any custom paintwork is to remove any emblems, nameplates or molding stripes on the car body in the area to be painted. These emblems or nameplates are often held on by nuts on the back side. If they are held on by push clips, you can remove them by prying carefully with a screwdriver or putty knife. On most late-model cars these emblems are secured by two-way tape which will pry off easily. Of course if you are painting a Lead Sled or custom, you have probably already removed the emblems and welded or leaded the holes closed.

in laying out the masking tape. The result, however, is well worth the effort.

The second trick is in using other colors to enhance the look of the flames so they appear to be more than a single dimension. Pinstriping around the flame outline does this to some extent by making it stand out from the background color.

More impressive, though, is the use of fogging. By lightly spraying another color overlapping the base color at either end of the flames or along the edges (or both), you can add texture and depth to the colors.

Planning your custom paint work is step one, and designing flames requires a hot touch. Ace custom painter Dave Bell calls this first step the laying out of the flames, and this phase offers an important insight into the techniques of a professional painter. To the pros, the preparation is everything. Flames are not just painted on a car; they are planned and laid out so the result is everything you hoped for.

Start planning your flames by checking out the designs on other cars. Look at all the pictures of hot rods wearing flames that you can find—from the traditional to the high tech.

The importance of good, thorough planning in designing a set of flames is shown in these three photographs of our project car, a 1952 Henry J—not your usual recipient of a flame job! The photo here shows the finished custom paint work: bright white flames turning to yellow to hot orange to red tips, all outlined in cobalt blue pinstriping. Envisioning such a final result requires thinking in reverse. Timothy Remus

Once you have decided on a design, take a couple pictures of your own project car, get the crayons or magic markers out and play. Draw in flames on the photograph and pay attention to where the lines will run in relation to the lines of your car. An alternative method is to photocopy the picture and draw on the black and white photocopy in color; the color will stand out and accentuate any mistakes you may be about to make.

Today, some master painters are designing their work on computer screens. The required computer hardware and software is expensive and often only practical for the professional. The equipment can perform some fancy work but only with a sharp designer running it. Just to make you feel better, remember that the early hot rodders had only their marking pens to work their magic.

The best results are achieved when you strive for simple design—just keep in the back of your mind that old 1940 Ford with flames built by Bob McCoy. The key to success is a good balance between design and color.

## Choosing colors: A rainbow of options

In the end, every set of flames is unique due to blends of color, choices of paint, designs and so on. The strength or impact of color depends upon three factors: hue, saturation and brightness. Hue is the basic property of the color that distinguishes one color from another. Saturation is the purity of hue or the degree to which a color is free from mixture with white. The brightness of a color is the characteristic we describe when we say a color is light or dark. Bright colors seem to reflect more light than dark ones.

It is possible to produce a pleasing effect from a mass of mixed colors, but you will achieve a more dramatic and probably more satisfactory result by restricting to one or two the number of hues that you use on your car. To dramatize the impact of the color you want, select an exceptionally pale or dark neutral base coat. A mass of complex elements within the paint scheme is as destructive as the use of too many hues. Each element will compete with the other for the viewer's attention.

Your reaction to a color depends not only on

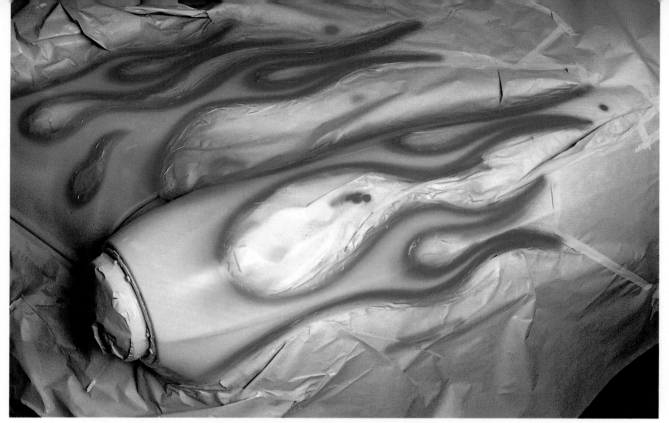

*Our project car several stages before completion with the masking tape and paper still in place. The red flame tips have just been sprayed on and the blue pinstriping comes next. Timothy Remus*

the color itself, but also on other colors near it. Red looks brighter and warmer when near blue. Blue, on the other hand, appears colder and more subdued when near red. This effect is called color contrast. Personal taste will largely determine which colors contrast and which colors clash, but a general rule applies: the more extreme the qualities between the two colors, the greater the contrast.

Harmony is possibly the most subtle and evocative of all the reactions among colors. Being creative, you can use it to establish the mood of your design. As clashing colors are often confusing, color harmony can create peace in your design—or it can be used to create disharmony.

To correct this, weaken the hue of the offending colors, or change colors altogether.

Armed with this information—and some good old-fashioned trial and error with your crayons and your pictures—you can achieve the exact color scheme you want when you paint your car. Make sure the strong area of contrast is the main area of your design, or at least related to it. It then will contribute to the design's composition without being too busy or distracting.

Remember, the only rule is that there are no rules. Experiment and experiment again with design and color—it's all in the best hot rodding tradition.

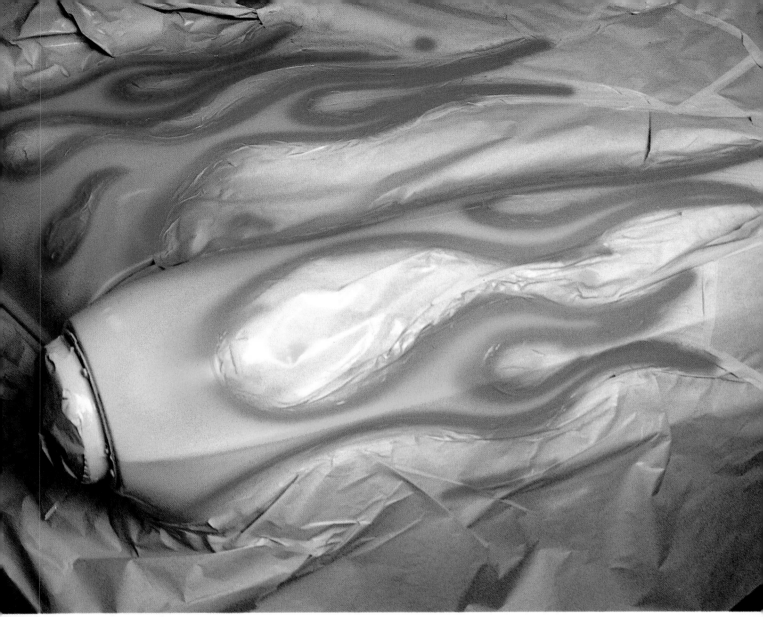

One stage earlier yet, before the red tips have been shot, showing the white base with yellow and orange built up around the edges. Looking backward through the project reveals the careful planning required to paint a professional set of flames. Timothy Remus

# Flames

# How to Paint Flames: Preparation

The secret to quality custom painting is not in the painting, as all the professionals will warn you. The secret lies in the preparation.

The first step when preparing your rod for painting is to remove any emblems, nameplates or molding. Chances are, with most hot rods these days, little in the way of molding is left on the car so this should get you ahead of the game right away.

The second step is to thoroughly clean your car. Paint does not adhere to wax or grease so you have to make certain to clean your car well. The automatic one dollar car wash or the neighborhood boy scouts' summer car wash doesn't count—it just won't do a good enough job. The

*With the flames laid out on the car, the masking tape is set down outlining the grease pencil's lines. Scotch Fine Line tape, manufactured by 3M, comes in widths from 1/16 to 1/2 inch. Most painters normally use 1/8 inch unless they need to make some unusually sharp corners. With a little practice you can make nice smooth curves—remember, practice makes perfect. Lay the tape down slowly, holding it in place every couple of inches. To make straight lines, just pull the tape out to the desired length and carefully stretch it tight but not taut so it snaps up again the moment you turn your back. Lay the end down where you want it and then run your finger along its length to stick it down. If you are not satisfied with the design simply pull up the tape and try again.*

trick is to use a wax or grease remover to cut through all those years of road tar.

**Sanding: Enough is never enough**

Now comes the time to flex your muscles and begin sanding. The bodywork must be free of flaws to provide a nice smooth surface for the paint. Sanding is the key, both in preparation for painting and between coats of primer and paint. Take the time at this stage to prepare the car right—if it's a job worth doing, it's worth doing right.

Sand until your shoulders are sore or until the electric sander is hot—and then do it over again. Even when the surface looks smooth unpainted, that lack of paint may be hiding defects. Those defects will stand out bright and shiny when your perfect coats of custom paint are dry.

For the pro, a well-prepped car body means no tiny dents, no waves, no scratches. When sanding keep the paper wet at all times. The reasons for using lots of water are simple: the water cuts down on the amount of clogging and encrustations on the face of the sandpaper, eliminates dust and, most importantly, leaves a smoother finish.

There are several important tricks to sanding as well, tricks they never taught you in high school shop class. If you are sanding by hand, keep your entire hand in contact with the surface of the car body and don't sand with just your

*Sandpaper is available in different grades with a numbering sequence running from coarse to fine to micro-fine grit. The lower the number, the more grit to the paper: here are sheets of 360, 600 and micro-fine 1500. Typically, the coarse paper is used first to remove large blemishes; finer papers are used to finish the surface. The backside of a sheet of sandpaper lists all of the paper's qualities, including a notation for wet-and-dry sandpaper, meaning it can be used with water. David H. Jacobs, Jr.*

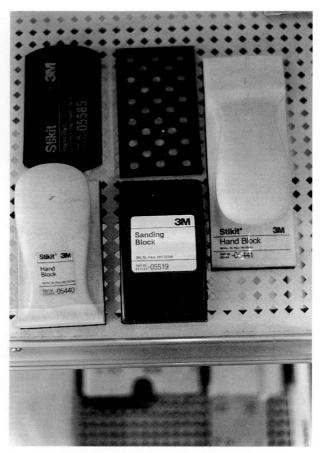

*Sanding blocks are almost mandatory for sanding down large expanses, such as fenders and the hood area when prepping for a flame job. The flat surface on a block prevents uneven sanding that occurs if you used solely your hand as backing. Different styles and shapes are available. David H. Jacobs, Jr.*

fingertips or the side of your palm. You'll get much more uniform results using the whole hand, and it's also less tiring on your hand.

There's one other bit of grandmotherly advice. Do not sand in circles, just as you never wax a car with a circular movement. No matter how conscientious you are about getting a smooth finish, those circular movements will show through the final coat of paint. Always sand in back and forth motions.

If you have chips or scratches in the base coat, pay special attention to featheredging these areas properly. Again, the smoothness of the bodywork is vital to the final product.

When you think you are finished, step back and take a last look at your handiwork. One final sanding is usually needed to make certain that all the panels are smooth. Use a finer grade of sandpaper for this last sanding to hone the finish.

The next step in a quality custom paint job seems to be overlooked by most how-to articles. The bare metal spots that you have so diligently sanded need to be treated so they don't rust as soon as you are finished applying your paint. Use a quality metal conditioner to remove and help neutralize rust. It will leave a dry, chemically clean, treated and etched surface that will promote paint adhesion and help prevent formation of any new rust.

## Masking: The flames become reality

Now you are ready to lay out the flames you

Scotch-Brite pads are ideal for scuffing up painted surfaces to give a rough surface for the new paint to adhere to. Surface prep work is essential to a good flame job so all of your hard work lasts and the paint bonds well with the metal. Scotch-Brite pads also can be used to prepare bumpers and trim pieces before custom painting. David H. Jacobs, Jr.

On this particular car there were some scratches on the right front fender that could be easily feathered out with either a DA sander or a sanding block using 180 grit sandpaper. Be certain to sand the scratches out completely, holding the block flat on the surface until you can feel no paint edge when you run your hand over the surface.

There are two different methods used to sand a vehicle before applying a flame paint job. Your first option is to sand the entire surface first, as we are doing on this 1953 Ford, then clear coat the entire vehicle. The second option is to lay out the tape stripes and sand and clear coat the flame pattern only. The advantage of clear coating the entire surface area is that you have no rough edges to catch and peel as the edges are sealed under the clear coat. Another plus is that clear coating the entire surface also adds gloss and depth to the other colors on the vehicle. If you choose not to clear coat the entire car, stay away from high-pressure car washes as they can quickly destroy your paint job by causing the edges to peel back. Carefully wet sand the entire area with 600 grit or finer wet or dry sandpaper; the 3M brand sandpaper found at your local auto parts store works well. Use a bucket of warm water and a sponge while sanding, and make certain to wipe the area dry occasionally to see how you are progressing. You only want to sand enough to provide a good base for paint adhesion—not to actually remove any paint film. One trick is to add a small amount of liquid dish-washing soap to the water to help lubricate the sandpaper, prevent it from clogging and make it last longer. When you have the body sanded correctly the entire surface will be dull with no shiny spots. Be careful when sanding near edges and body lines so you don't sand through the paint film—it's easy to do! You may want to use a 3M Scotch-Brite pad in these areas; it will dull the paint without actually removing it. The pad is flexible so it works nicely in tight areas that are hard to reach with normal sandpaper.

*When prepping the body for a flame job or any other custom painting, it is essential to sand down all surfaces—including the tough-to-reach creases and character lines on some cars. Sanding inside this grooved section is almost impossible with a sanding block or electric sander. Here, a wooden paint stir stick is used as the sanding block; in especially tight areas, your fingers may be the best medium to hold the sandpaper. David H. Jacobs, Jr.*

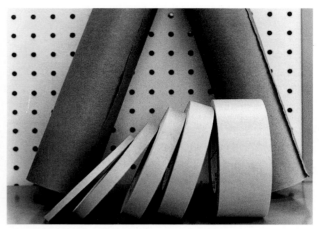

*Automotive masking tape and masking paper are designed specifically for use on auto paint projects such as flame jobs and other custom painting. Neither paint nor solvent will penetrate the products, and the adhesive on the tape will not stay on the surface after the tape is removed. Other types of masking paper— newspaper, typing paper and so on—may allow the paint to soak through as they are made of thinner paper stock. Use the right stuff! You should have several rolls of masking tape on hand when starting your flame work: a roll of ¾ inch tape, two inch tape and ⅛ inch tape for laying the intricate curves of the flames. David H. Jacobs, Jr.*

have designed onto your car. For many people this is the fun part—and with reason. Suddenly, after all the planning and preparation, the design begins to take form.

One route for laying out the lines of the flames is to use a grease pencil to draw directly onto the car. Another way is to start with the masking tape. Transfer your design onto the car and mask the shapes.

## Masking tapes and paper

In choosing masking tape, the best bet is to buy a new roll for use in your special flames job. Masking tape has a tendency to go brittle with age, resulting in a flaking, crusty feeling that does little in masking out overspray or even

adhering to surfaces. Fresh tape is easily identified: it is supple, bends easy and is almost spongy between your fingers. The 3M company makes about the best masking tape for your money.

Masking tape comes in several widths valuable to the flames painter, ranging from the thinnest at ⅛ inch on up to two inches. For the initial laying out of the flames, use the ⅛ inch masking tape. It bends easily and can be laid to follow the nice, smooth curves and contours you will want in your flames.

Holding the roll of tape with one hand, use your other hand to position the tape on the body panel to be painted, tacking it down lightly as you go. For best results—that is, smoother curves—move quickly. If you lay the tape at a slow, cautious pace, you are certain to get wavy lines; laying the tape quickly will result in smoother lines. And remember, if you don't like the line you tacked down, simply pull the tape up and start afresh.

After the ⅛ inch tape is laid down to your satisfaction, run your finger along it to smooth it in between the spaces where you tacked it down. Then take a popsicle stick or tongue depresser and press the tape so it will not peel away. Use the stick along the edges of the tape as well to

*Now the fun starts. Eric Aurand draws the flames on the hood and fenders of our project car, a 1952 Henry J. Here, he is drawing the flames freehand, using a grease pencil. Some painters prefer to use the grease pencil to lay out their preliminary flame designs; others prefer to go directly to the taping. It's truly a matter of preference, although for the beginner, the grease pencil may be easier and more simple to use. Timothy Remus*

*Now is the time to lay out the flames on the other side of the car if you want the flames to be symmetrical. Again there are a couple different ways to do this. You can either do a lot of careful measuring and walking back and forth from side to side or you can make a paper pattern to transfer the design to the other side of the car. This is obviously the easier route—and will save your feet. Lay the paper on the car and fasten it temporarily with some masking tape. Either trace the pattern with a pencil or use the upraised edges of the tape to rub a crayon over and make a rubbing. Remove the paper and place it on a relatively soft surface such as a piece of cardboard or fiberboard. Using a pounce wheel, follow the outline of the design; the pounce wheel will perforate the paper with small holes. Fill a small cloth bag with a powder such as baby powder or household baking flour for dark-colored cars or charcoal powder on light-colored ones. Punch a single small hole in the bag and pat it along the perforations in your design. The powder will leave a series of small dots after the paper is removed. Using your ⅛ inch masking tape follow the dots and you will have matching flames on both sides of the car. Another way to do this is to cut out the design and use the shape as a stencil. Secure the paper on the opposite side of the car, using reference points to make sure that the flames line up in the same place as on the other side.*

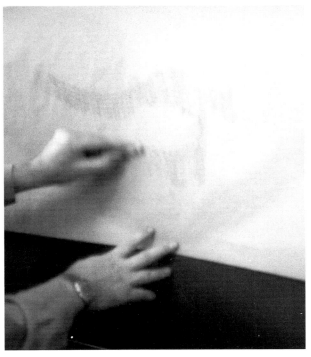

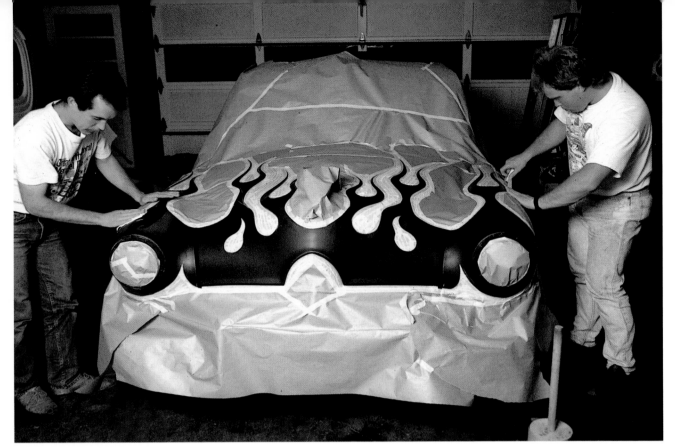

Be liberal with the use of masking tape and masking paper to fill in and cover all areas you do not want painted. With our project car, virtually the whole car was masked off—the right way to do it if you want professional results. Timothy Remus

*Previous page*

*Using the fine line tape as a guide, Jeff Teig begins to mask off the parts of the car that are not to be painted and to protect from overspray. Make certain that all edges of the tape are pressed down tight or you will have paint creeping and running underneath. Remember that the overspray will get everywhere you don't want it to go! Timothy Remus*

make certain the tape is solidly affixed; any gaps or loose spots along that edge will result in blurred, indistinct paint lines.

With the fine tape laid down, use a thicker tape of between ¾ inch and one inch in width, following over the outside edge of the thin tape. Since the thin tape is more delicate, this thicker tape will make sure the ⅛ inch does not accidently get torn or caught on something.

Now use your ¾ inch tape to set the masking paper in place. Nothing works better than true masking paper. Although it isn't free the way butcher paper or day-old newspaper is, the cost is worth it in protecting your car from overspray or the ink that can come off the newspaper.

You can tear or cut the masking paper into strips to tape it down in between the flames, and then use the sheets around the edges. Try not to get any folds or humps in the paper as you lay it. Folds can catch overspray and splatter it on the newly painted surface when you pull it up. Humps in the paper can act like miniature ski slopes, letting overspray run down the sides and directly onto the surface.

In general, mask at least three feet in every direction away from the custom painting you are doing. Overspray will get everywhere and anywhere you don't want it. A little extra expense in buying masking paper and tape will be worth it. Better safe than sorry—especially where paint is concerned.

Like sanding, good masking and laying out of the taped flames is the key to the final product. Hard work, foresight and patience are the virtues here.

**Laying out symmetrical flames**

A large custom paint scheme such as flames often looks best when symmetrical from side to side of the car—especially on the hood or front

51

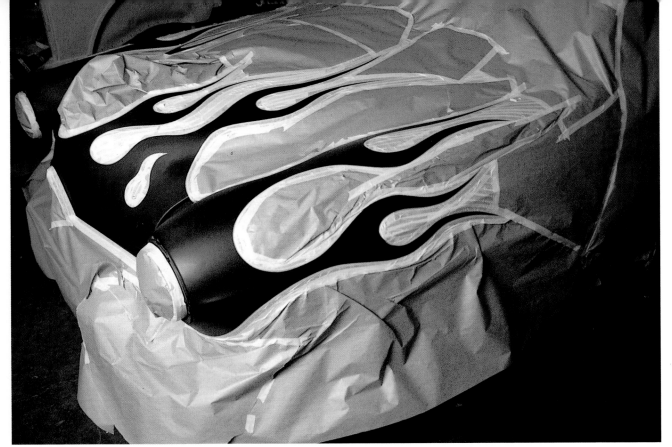

The front fender of our project car prepped, masked and ready for painting. Prior to actually shooting the paint, the flame area should be wiped down one last time with a tack cloth to remove any dust or static. On fiberglass-bodied cars, static can be an especially worrisome problem. One solution is to wipe down the surface with rubbing alcohol, which aids in removing static. Timothy Remus

end where both sides of the design can be seen at the same time.

The trick to symmetry is to lay out one side of the car's design using chalk or a marker, cover those lines with ⅛ inch masking tape, and then tape a large piece of paper on top. Use a crayon or piece of chalk to rub the outline of the tape flames onto the paper. When complete, remove the rubbing and cut out the flames from the paper. This is now your stencil to lay out an identical symmetrical design on the other side of the car.

The final step before you start painting is to mask off the rest of the car from any overspray. Beware! The overspray is insidious and it will go everywhere you haven't protected.

*Previous page*

*With the car properly masked off, the next step is essential to prevent rust from forming underneath your new paint—a little extra effort here can mean years of added paint life! Treat the bare metal spots with a metal conditioner such as Ditzler's Metal Prep DX579 or DuPont's 5717 S Metal Conditioner. Metal conditioners remove and help neutralize rust, leaving a dry, chemically clean treated and etched surface that promotes paint adhesion and helps prevent formation of new rust. Metal conditioner is a mild acid, so follow the manufacturer's instructions carefully. Brush or wipe the metal prep onto the bare metal, let it sit a few minutes and then wipe dry with a clean cotton cloth. If the conditioner dries before you are through, rewet the surface and dry it again. Wait the recommended time and then apply a primer surfacer. Timothy Remus*

## Degreasing and final sanding

Once you have the flames laid out and the masking in place, go over the surface to be painted with a degreaser. Degreasing helps the paint stick.

Finally, make one last pass at the surface with a sheet of dry sandpaper or a Scotch-Brite pad. Roughing up the surface so the paint adheres will ensure a long life for the paintwork.

The last step before mixing up your paint is to clean away any dust or sanding residue with a couple blasts from an air compressor. Make certain to get at the edges of the masking tape so there is nothing to prevent a clean, crisp border around the flames.

# Flames

# How to Paint Flames: Painting

Maestro hot rodders such as Jim "Jake" Jacobs and Pete Chapouris of Pete and Jake Hot Rod Repairs fame are prime (no pun intended) examples of creativity when it comes to handling a spray gun. Their handiwork has set new standards in the hot rodding business, but most of all it offers a lesson: creativity and imagination are the only things holding you back. The spectacular set of flames on Pete and pal Jerry Slover's "California Kid" hot rod is an example. And as all hot rodders know—from Pete and Jake to those working out of their own garages—when it comes to making a rod truly hot, paint is magic.

Money, in the 1950s as today, is one of the factors involved when you decide what type of custom paint to apply to your car and whether you're going to do it yourself or have someone else do it. Remember, professional standards yield professional results—either in your garage or in a commercial paint booth.

The early hot rodders and customizers had to learn their trade the hard way, either by working an apprenticeship for an expert or by trial and error—the school of hard knocks and paint splotches. If you are willing to learn and practice, there is only a short step between the beginner and the expert.

## Safety equipment for painting

There are three basic tools you need to paint flames: masking tape, safety equipment and paint. There are different types of masking tapes and different routes you can go with different kinds of paint, but there is no substitute for breathing masks and eye protection.

There are some painters—both pros and amateurs—who come from the old school of painting and never use safety breathing equipment. Many of them started painting in "the old days" before the dangers of paint fumes, solvents and binders were understood. Many of these painters continue this way today, even when the dangers are well-known.

If you are painting with lacquer, enamel or urethane, or using an aerosol spray can, airbrush or spray gun to paint, you must wear a mask—in other words, at all times. The masks cost little, especially considered in the light of your own health. Filter safety masks from 3M sell for $10 or less and work fine in blocking paint vapors

*Now you are ready to mix up a little of the base coat color. Stir the paint thoroughly for several minutes with a mixing stick, especially if it is a metallic color as the metallic particles tend to settle toward the bottom of the can before you know it. Strain the paint into the cup using a medium- or fine-mesh strainer. Most paint stores will give you free strainers and stir sticks when you purchase your supplies. Thin the paint the recommended amount, generally 100 to 150 percent with a quality lacquer thinner. Timothy Remus*

54

Perhaps the most important step in custom painting is not prepping the car but prepping yourself in terms of safety and protection from the chemicals you will be using. Here is a selection of filter respirators available at an auto paint store. Some filters are designed to be exposed to outside air for 40 hours and then disposed of. To keep them in good condition, they are enclosed in a resealable plastic bag. If you don't choose to purchase a respirator, at least buy a package of 3M filter masks. David H. Jacobs, Jr.

A Sharpe detail paint gun, just one of several brands and types of spray guns available. A standard air gun is ideal for the major portion of your flame painting, such as the base white paint on our project car. From there, a touch-up detail gun such as this or an airbrush work well to fog in the border colors and flame tips. There is a spray gun for all jobs and for everyone, whether you are a professional or a beginner. David H. Jacobs, Jr.

The first step is to apply three to four coats of a good lacquer-type primer surfacer, waiting several minutes between coats to allow the solvents to "flash"—chemistry talk for letting the thinners evaporate. Ditzler's Kondar acrylic primer surfacer—DZ-3 light gray or DZ-7 red oxide—is a fast-building easy-sanding primer with excellent adhesion qualities. Thin the primer using the required amount of lacquer thinner recommended by the manufacturer. Ditzler recommends using its DTL 16 thinner. You need to apply enough primer surfacer to build up the bare metal areas to the level of the surrounding paint surfaces. An optional step is the application of a primer sealer such as Ditzler Sealer 70 (DL1970). The reason for using sealer is to help hold down sand scratches, prime any bare metal spots that may remain and help the top coat color to hold out. Do not thin sealers, however—they are ready to spray as they come from the can.

from invading your lungs. If you really want to ensure your health, respirator masks are available as well, selling usually in the $30 to $50 range.

## Setting up for painting

Whether you are a novice or an expert in painting, you have to start at the beginning. The first step is to obtain the proper tools and learn how to use them. Then, it's a good idea to familiarize yourself with the painting product available to you. The next step is to practice on a panel before attempting to do the whole car.

Paint can be applied in many different ways. In early days, the backyard hot rodders sometimes used vacuum cleaners turned on reverse, while many a shadetree painter has performed feats of artistry with spray cans bought from the local auto parts store. Others armed themselves

Primer-surfacer from DuPont: on the left, grey acrylic and on the right, red oxide acrylic. Typically, the rule is that for light colors of paint, a light-colored primer is used—such as this grey. For dark paints, the dark primer provides a darker background. Loaded with high solid contents, primer-surfacers fill in light sanding scratches and other blemishes. When dry, the surface can be sanded with 300 or 400 grit sandpaper for a smooth texture ready to paint. David H. Jacobs, Jr.

Pearl colors add depth to custom paint work—especially flames. Pearl additives are somewhat similar to metal flakes except that they are much smaller—so small, in fact, that they are contained in a pastelike solution. Pearls come in different colors, and are produced by almost all paint manufacturers for use with their paint systems. Shown here are pearl solutions from SEM and PPG. David H. Jacobs, Jr.

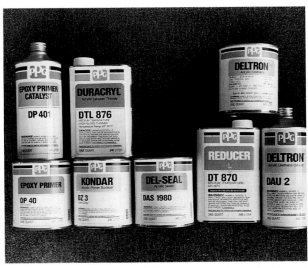

It is essential that you stick to just one brand of paint system throughout your flame job; this is the system from PPG. All of these products are compatible with each other but may not be with similar products from other manufacturers! The PPG system includes, from left to right: epoxy primer and catalyst; primer-surfacer and lacquer thinner; acrylic sealer; and acrylic urethane paint, reducer and catalyst. David H. Jacobs, Jr.

Metal flakes can be added to clear paint to give paint finishes a sparkle appearance. To keep metal flakes evenly suspended in paint gun cups for an even finish, many custom painters put a couple ball bearings or marbles in the cup and then shake the gun after each paint pass. Mixing directions for the paint and metal flake solution, and air compressor and paint gun settings, must be followed to the letter on the individual cans for a professional-looking metallic finish. David H. Jacobs, Jr.

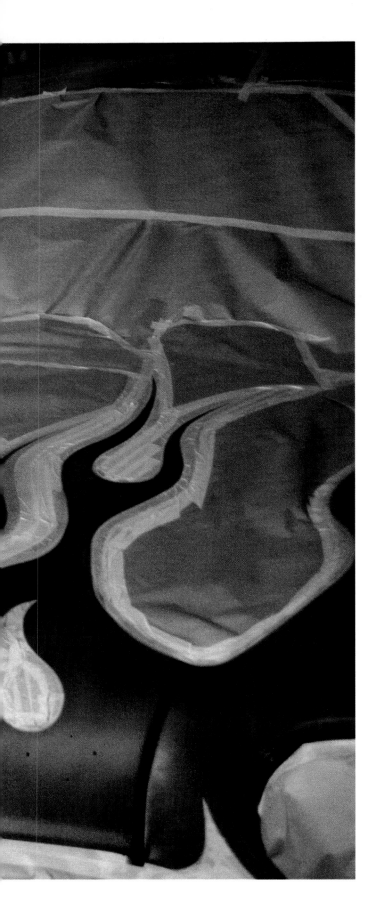

with an arsenal of different-sized paintbrushes—or even dipped the whole body into a vat of paint, as at the original factory. Today, most people use a spray gun.

The tools you will need include a siphon-feed quality paint gun, air compressor, air hose, couplers, filters and an exhaust fan if you are working indoors. These tools can be purchased, rented or borrowed.

## Choosing painting approaches

There are basically two routes to go in choosing painting approaches for spraying your set of custom flames. The first is the true amateur's route: prepackaged aerosol cans of spray paints. The second is the use of spray guns or airbrushes and compressors. Both have their benefits.

### Spray cans

Spray cans are cheap but not necessarily easy to use. You can buy aerosol spray cans at most auto parts stores for a minimum of money. The paint is available in a huge array of colors and several styles of paint, from enamel to lacquer. Trick paints such as pearls, candies and some metalflakes are often available.

The major problem with spray cans is in the spray pattern they produce. As the cans are made to use once and then throw away, the nozzles are made to do the job and not much more. Thus the pattern is usually a circle and not an oval-shaped field with the paint concentrated in a regulated pattern.

So while the spray cans are cheap, getting a professional-quality job from an aerosol can often requires more expertise than even the pro has. Still, they do work, and with practice you can do good work in a minimal amount of time with little effort.

### Spray guns

Spray gun is a general term comprising several different styles of paint guns used for differ-

*Now it's time for the main color—a bright white in this case. Before you start spraying the car make certain your spray gun has a nice even pattern by spraying a test pattern on a junk fender, a piece of spare metal or some masking paper. Candy colors are transparent so it is very easy to get a streaky or blotchy looking paint job if your gun is not working properly or if you do not apply the paint evenly. Thin the lacquer according to the manufacturer's recommendations, then apply several coats of lacquer until you get the desired coverage you want. The more coats you apply the darker the color you will get. When using lacquer hold your spray gun six to eight inches from the surface being painted to achieve a nice even pattern. Timothy Remus*

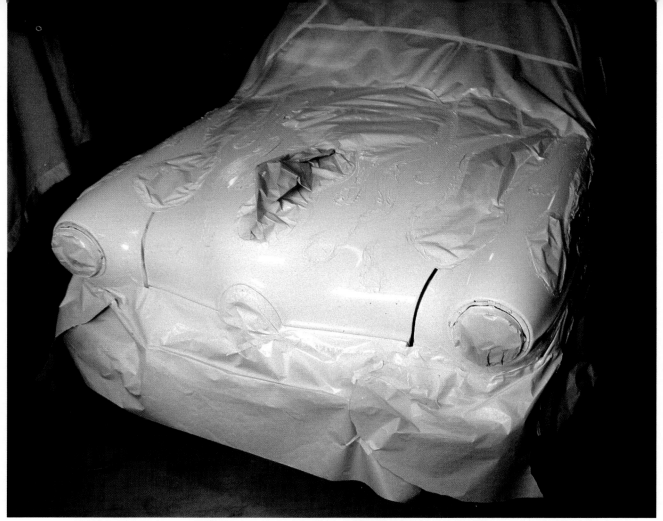

*The desired strength of our base bright white color has been achieved with several coats of paint. Now the paint is allowed to sit overnight—at the least—to let the base dry before the other colors are applied. When finished spraying, clean out your air gun right away and don't let the paint inside gum up the intricate workings. Timothy Remus*

ent jobs by painters of varying scales of expertise. Basically, there is a spray gun for all jobs and for everyone, whether you are a professional or a beginner.

A standard air gun is ideal for big painting and custom painting jobs. They cover larger areas in a shorter amount of time.

Touch-up guns have a more limited spray pattern, so they are smaller and slower but offer more control to the amateur in painting. Touch-up guns can operate with smaller air compressors than those required for the larger, standard air guns.

Airbrushes are the easiest to use for the novice. They offer a smaller spray pattern, better control and limited overspray. You can either do the complete flames job with an airbrush or use one after the standard air gun to blend colors or add flame tips or fogging along the edges. The air compressor needed to power an airbrush can be small.

There are numerous types, makes and qualities of air guns, touch-up guns and airbrushes available. Shop around for prices and packages to see what is on the market. Also ask your friends what they have had good luck using. Brand names such as Badger, Binks, or Devilbiss are quality units to keep an eye out for.

**Air compressors**

You can either purchase or rent air compressors, depending on whether you are doing just one flame job or planning on doing several jobs. For all jobs, an air compressor with at least one horsepower is required; five horsepower or more is ideal with larger air guns. Many air compressors run on the normal household 110 volts; the

Using a small airbrush for the detail work, Eric begins to apply the bright yellow paint to the outlying edges of the flames. Orange and red coats will be added to the tips, but it is important to thoroughly cover the edges of the flames here and let the other coats of paint build up on top of the yellow for an even finish. Timothy Remus

higher-powered compressors use 220 volts, and this is what you'll want if you are doing more than a weekend job.

As with spray guns, there are numerous air compressors available. Good units are usually on sale at Sears, Montgomery Ward or other retail stores.

## Working with a spray gun

As custom painting is an art, the spray gun is the medium to master in becoming the artist. For starters, try the gun out by shooting some practice strokes at a piece of scrap metal. This is ideal for working on your technique, but it also is important to do each time you start your gun up to make certain there are no paint blobs waiting in the nozzle to splatter all over your nicely prepared panel.

There are several "always" involved in painting with a spray gun:

• *Always* hold the spray gun perpendicular to the surface you are painting. Tilting the gun up or down on the vertical axis will give an uneven paint pattern, concentrating too much paint at the top if you are aiming down and vice versa. That extra paint is sure to run.

• *Always* move the gun in a straight plane following the contour of the panel you are painting. If you hold your arm in one place and pivot your wrist with the spray gun, you will shoot uneven coats on the surface. Keep your wrist flexible.

• *Always* hold the spray gun between six and eight inches from the surface. Hold the gun too close and the paint will shoot too hard against the surface, adhering heavy and sagging. Hold the gun too far away and it won't hit the surface hard

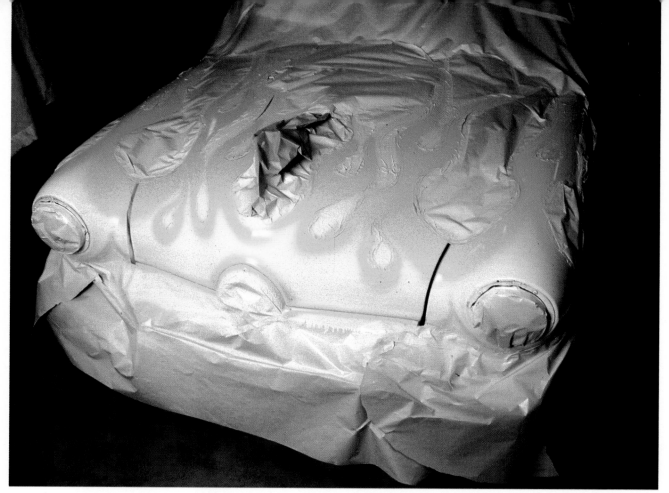

*The yellow flame edges and base around the grille have been airbrushed on top of the white base coat and are allowed to dry at least overnight. Don't rush the drying time—even with lacquer or urethane—as nowhere else in life does the maxim, Haste makes waste, hold truer than in custom painting. Timothy Remus*

enough; the finish will be dusty and sandy. The spray pattern is designed for a set distance and will give that nice, regular oval-shaped pattern only at that distance. Paint runs, inconsistent coverage or an orange-peel finish are all probable results of failing on your distance.

• *Some final always:* In painting a panel, shoot the paint in alternate left and right strokes. Trigger the spray gun at the start and finish of each stroke, minimizing overspray. Each stroke should overlap the one above or below it by half of the spray gun's paint pattern. In painting large expanses, it is best to break up the panel and spray it in sections of between 24 and 36 inches in width.

## Choosing paints: Types and properties

There are numerous types of modern paints available, including acrylic enamel, acrylic lacquer and urethane paints. (Of course, if you want to be old-fashioned or traditional to a fault, there is always alkyd enamel and nitrocellulose lacquer.) Naturally, each paint type has its own pros and cons.

The two basic types of paints are enamels and lacquers. Within each type there are several different specialty paints designed for professional uses.

The major difference between enamels and lacquers lies in their chemical make-up and how they work on your car. Paint has three main ingredients: binders, pigments and solvents. Af-

*Next page*

*The orange trim is added over the yellow, leaving an overlap that allows the colors to blend together when finished. While the white base paint is a lacquer, we used One Shot sign painter's enamel for the yellow, orange and red trim colors! One Shot is an inert paint, chemically designed so that it will not react with the other lacquer paint used on the car. Timothy Remus*

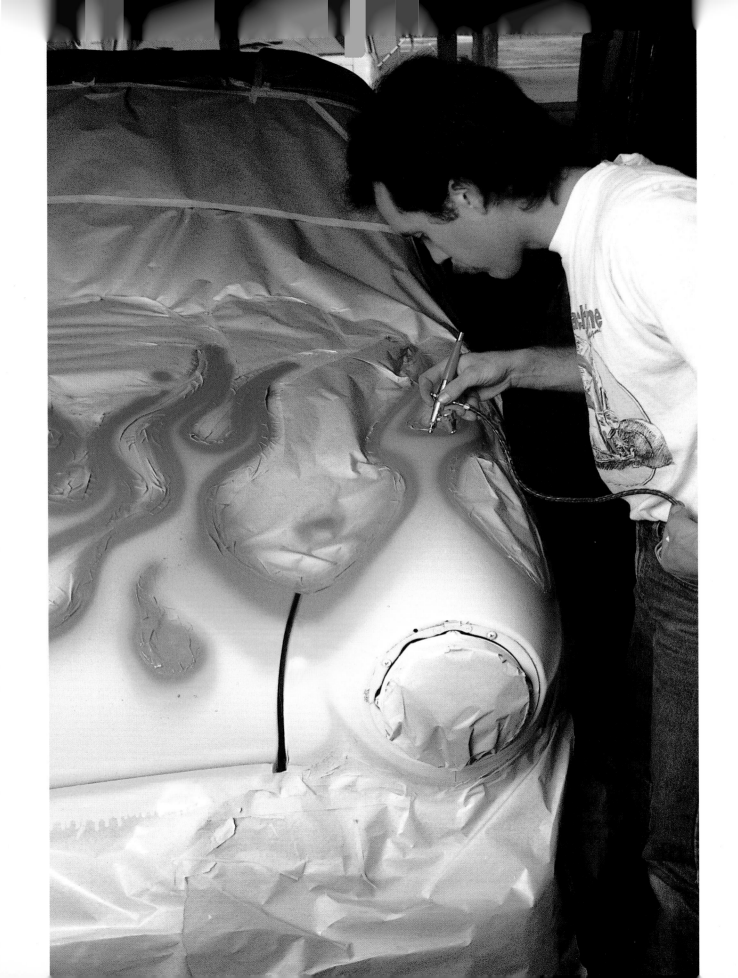

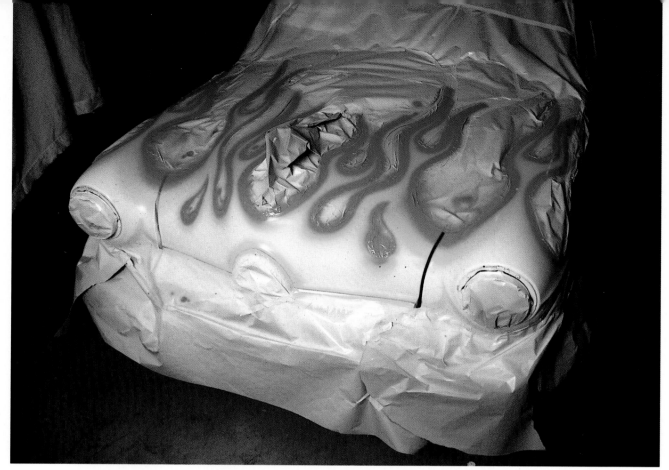

*The orange is now allowed to dry overnight. The key to a good traditional flame job is to gently blend the edges of the colors together to breathe life into the fire. Care when overlapping the paint is the trick.* Timothy Remus

ter the paint has been applied to a surface and the solvents have evaporated, the part of the coating that remains on the surface and changes to a solid film is the binder. Enamels are based on varnish-type binders and dry in a two-step process, thus taking longer to dry. Lacquers, on the other hand, dry by evaporation of the solvent it is based in; they dry much quicker than enamels and so may be better suited to your custom painting.

### Enamel paints

Enamel is less expensive to use than most of the other paints. It adheres well to most surfaces and requires minimal surface preparation. It does have its problems, however. Enamel takes a long time to dry and so it must be applied in light coats to prevent running or sagging. The slow drying time also allows dirt, dust and insects ample time to settle.

Enamel is typically a thicker paint than lacquer, and two coats of enamel will give about the same coverage as five to six coats of lacquer. This difference in coverage is something to consider when looking at the amount of time needed in painting and the weight the materials will lift from your billfold.

Enamel can be sprayed over a lacquer finish without a problem, but lacquer cannot be sprayed on top of enamel as it will not adhere.

### Acrylic enamel paints

Acrylic enamel is one of the modern high-tech paints, and is also one of the most durable and weather resistant. The paint is also fixed with chemicals to provide a high-gloss finish. Acrylic enamel has a much quicker drying time than enamel, and once dry, resists scratches better.

Acrylic enamel basically adds liquid plastic—acrylic—to the regular enamel paint as a binder instead of the standard nitrocellulose. This liquid plastic is naturally harder and more durable than the standard binder.

When painting with acrylic enamel, good dust control is essential; otherwise, the paint will attract dust particles that will settle on the freshly painted finish.

Acrylic enamel is a thick, rich paint and

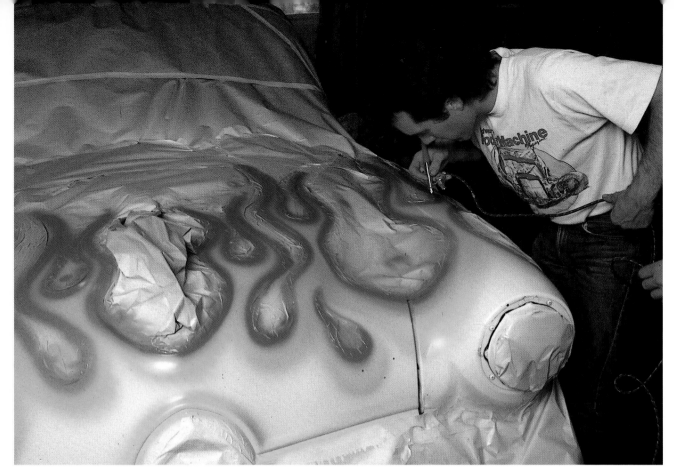

*The airbrush work becomes more precise and time-consuming as Eric applies the final red edge to the flame tips. With this layer of paint, more of the red* *ends up on the masking tape and paper so that the flame edges are thin, giving definition to the blend of colors. Timothy Remus*

when sprayed on a surface, it provides good coverage, tending to fill in well. A popular myth, however, is that paint fills minor imperfections on the surface. Don't believe it. Any imperfections are actually accentuated by the paint!

Acrylic enamel also resists ultraviolet radiation and is widely available in a variety of colors.

### Nitrocellulose lacquer paints

Once upon a time, lacquer was the wonder paint used on most every custom-painted car. Today, that place has been taken over by acrylic lacquer and lacquer has fallen by the wayside.

Lacquer does not contain oils and cannot withstand wide ranges in temperature or hard bumps and knocks. Therefore lacquer must have plasticizers added to it to keep the film permanently flexible. Catalysts may also be added to the paint to make the liquid coating convert to a solid more effectively.

### Acrylic lacquer paints

As with acrylic enamel, acrylic lacquer adds

the liquid plastic binder to the regular lacquer paint, providing a harder, more durable lacquer finish.

Acrylic lacquer offers improved ultraviolet radiation protection, meaning the paint will fade slower than regular lacquer if left out in the sun. It also is easy to apply and dries almost instantly.

Acrylic lacquer can be applied nearly anywhere without worrying about having a paint booth to paint in or having to wear special paint spray respirators to protect your health. If you choose one of the new paints that requires additives containing isocyanates, however, make sure you use proper respiration equipment and work only in a properly ventilated area.

While acrylic enamel dries to a good shine on its own, to reach the high-gloss finish many customizers and show car painters desire, lacquer mut be rubbed, buffed out and compounded to bring the shine to the forefront. Thus, lacquer requires a lot of extra work—both in application and in elbow grease later on. The end result is well worth the effort, however, and nothing

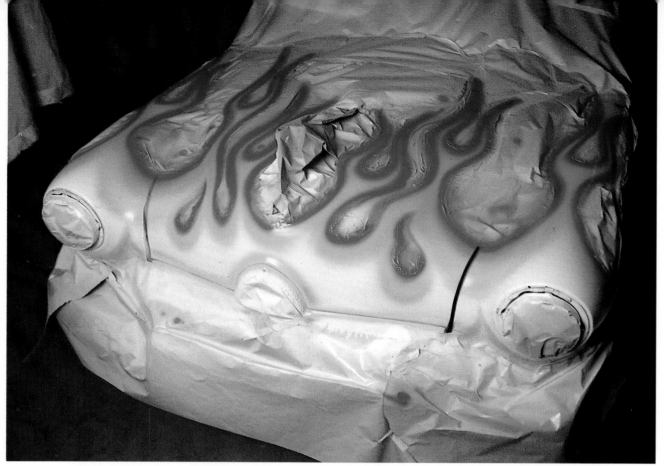

*Base white coat, three applications of colors and the spray gun work is finished. After allowing the final red* *paint to dry overnight, the masking paper and tape can be carefully removed. Timothy Remus*

matches a well-rubbed lacquer finish for depth, clarity and shine.

A wide variety of acrylic lacquer colors are readily available.

### Urethane paints

Urethane is an enamel by make-up, but not by the way it sprays and adheres. Because of this feature, it is ideal for undercarriages. Urethane is without a doubt the toughest finish, but also the most expensive.

When urethanes were first introduced, color availability was limited. Now, however, virtually any color is available.

### Color types

There are three basic types of paint colors you can use when doing flames: solids, metallics and glamour colors such as candies, pearls, metalflakes and so on. Remember that each of the three types has its own advantages and drawbacks.

Standard colors often must be brightened up or defined with some kind of trim or pinstriping.

Metallic colors are good for all-around use. Candy and pearl colors are brilliant and beautiful but are more prone to fading. Many pros prefer a candy color because they like the depth and brilliance that only candy colors have. In choosing the type of paint for your paint job, therefore, you have to consider how you use your car.

### Pinstriping methods

There are three routes you may take in pinstriping. First, you can purchase adhesive pinstriping tape from auto parts stores and lay it out easily and quickly—although perhaps not as nicely.

Second, you can use a pinstriping machine, which you fill with paint and run along the surface. The machine is designed to regulate its paint flow and provides a nice, even stripe.

And finally, there is the old pro's method—a long-bristled brush and sign-painter's paint. The job requires a steady hand, lots of practice and lots of time, but the results are certainly worth the extra effort.

We chose to mix lacquer with enamel paint, but if you stick strictly to one type of paint, usually lacquer, the final step is to apply a few coats of clear lacquer to protect the colors and give you some material to color sand and rub to bring out the shine. On another project car, we mixed up some clear acrylic lacquer, such as Ditzler's Duracryl DCA-468 Hi-Performance Clear, and thinned it 150 to 200 percent with a good lacquer thinner such as Ditzler's DTL-876. Tack off the surface, then apply three or four coats, again waiting several minutes between coats for the thinners to flash.

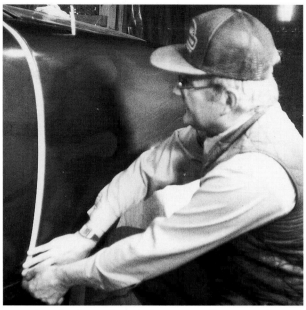

Here is a little trick to help prevent burning through the paint on the edges of adjacent panels when you are buffing with a machine. Tape a piece of ¾ inch masking tape to the edge of the adjacent panel, tucking the edge of the tape into the opening between the two panels. Now when you buff near the edge with your machine it will hit the tape instead of the paint on the other panel.

After proper drying time—usually overnight if you can be patient—color sand the area with 1000 grit ultra-fine wet-and-dry sandpaper. Dip the sandpaper in water and then use a sponge or wet cloth to wet the spot you need to sand. Wet sand the area paying particular attention to smoothing the edge left by the masking tape. Be careful not to sand through the clear coat. The results will begin to surface slowly and surely. Color sanding is the key to bringing out the highlights of your labor.

Now hand or machine rub the area using a heavy-duty rubbing compound, like Ditzler's Pastel Compound Fast Cut DRX 55, until you achieve the desired gloss. You can do the entire job by hand but it is a lot of work. Even using a machine to rub, you will need to do lots of hand rubbing anyway to get into tight corners that the machine can't reach. Be careful to stay away from body lines and edges—the machine can burn through the paint finish before you know it.

Jeff stripes the front of our Henry J. One Shot enamel paint is the key to fine pinstriping work for the beginner or amateur. The paint can be simply whipped away with a rag if the line you paint is not to your liking. The enamel base of the paint is the trick—with its slow drying time compared to lacquer, the enamel remains wet and solvent for at least five to ten minutes, giving you ample time to survey your work and change your mind. Timothy Remus

Previous page

Pinstriping the edge of your flames may be the most difficult part of the entire job, but there are many professional stripers who will be happy to do the job for you. If you're going to do the job yourself, Sign Painters One Shot lettering enamel and the long sword-type brush work well. One Shot lettering enamel is currently available in 26 colors—from there, you can mix the colors to make virtually any other hue you may want. Another alternative is to use a tape stripe such as a 3M Scotchcal which comes in a variety of widths and colors. Although upon close inspection they do not look as professional as a hand-painted stripe, from a few feet away you can't tell the difference. Here, Eric begins striping our project car with cobalt blue One Shot enamel. Timothy Remus

Eric stripes the flowing flames running along the fenders of the Henry J. The long bristles of a pinstriping brush aid in making a single, continuous stripe to run the length of a flame without interruption. The long bristles can hold an ample amount of paint, but it is important to dip the brush into the paint at the start of each stripe. Timothy Remus

Tools of the pinstriping trade. From top to bottom: Beugler pinstriping tool, a roll of magnetic guide tape, artist's lettering brushes and three dry pinstripe brushes. The car hood here was an ideal practice palate for the amateur pinstriper. Practice also includes adjusting paint and solvent mixtures in order to arrive at a good consistency of paint that will flow easily and not run. David H. Jacobs, Jr.

Previous page

The complete pinstriping job can be the most time-consuming and labor-intensive part of the flame custom painting. Patience and long, careful hours are required if you're going to do it yourself. Other options are always available, including the use of pinstriping tape or simply hiring the job out to a professional pinstriper. Timothy Remus

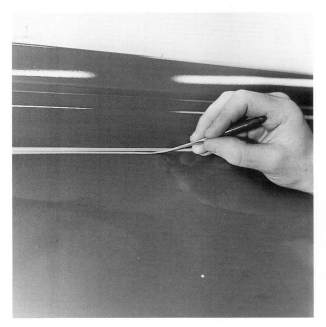

The key to fine pinstriping is a steady hand. The brush is held firmly between your fingers like a pen or pencil but instead of bending your wrist as you paint, your entire arm must move to give long, even strokes. The width of the pinstripe can be slightly altered by pushing the brush harder onto the surface. If only the tip of the brush makes contact, the pinstripes will be thin, and vice versa. Thus, another concern in pinstriping is to keep your pressure on the brush constant. David H. Jacobs, Jr.

To some hot rodders, pinstripes make the flames. We chose this traditional design of white flames blending to red with the cobalt blue outline to accentuate and define the design. Truly a hot Henry J! Timothy Remus

# Flames

## The Modern Look

From the Bonneville Salt Flats to the dry lakes of southern California to the Saturday night drive-ins of the Midwest, flames and scallops have marked hot rods and let the whole world know who was coming to town.

Traditionally, the hot rodders' paint designs consisted of a single theme. Not today. Custom painting has come a long way since the early days of rodding—perhaps further than any other part of the hobby! Advances in paint technology have given us new paints that are stronger, more glossy and easier to apply than ever before. Computers are allowing some on the forefront of customizing to perform new tricks. And the hot styles of graphics and neon colors are starting a revolution in rodding. Today, anything goes.

The hottest trend is certainly the use of graphics. The designs may be a wave of colors or just a splash of a single color, splatters or blobs of paint, artistic brush strokes or a sole line of pinstriping—even a miniature cartoon of a surfer riding out the stripe!

The most fascinating side of the new graphics trends is that flames have held their own and have even been incorporated in the new designs. Scallops and flames are back with wilder designs, swirls of scrollwork and futuristic forms. Flames are burning in colors never seen in your average fireplace—green, blue, violet, hot pink and more. The current trend is: if it looks good, do it!

*Whether you call him the Mad Hatter or the Wizard, he's known among the painting circuit as the homeless Mark Fenyo. Here he is striping a red 1936 Chevrolet. Fenyo carries his paints, brushes and supplies in a little red wagon. The only difference between a man and a boy might be the price of his toys, but Mark uses a toy wagon as a tool of his trade.*

74

Hot rodding legend has it that flames were developed from scallop designs used on airplane racers and track racers. In the 1980s, scallops have been revived—but they're far removed from the scallops the 1950s hot rodders used! Scallops generally were long, narrow, tapering panels that followed the contours of the car, usually originating toward the front and sweeping to the rear where they tapered to a point. This 1933 Ford three-window Highboy Coupe owned by Bill and Shirley Schneider of Belmond, Iowa, is about as radical as you could dream of with scallops. The base body paint is brilliant yellow highlighted with fuchsia scallops. Blue pinstriping highlights the scalloping. The Schneiders continued their revival and reformation of the traditional scallop job by painting the grille, wheel centers and headlight buckets to match the fuchsia scalloping.

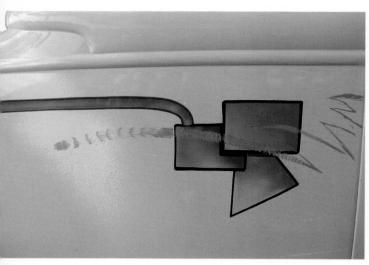

*A detail shot showing off some of the modern look in graphics. This bright yellow Model A Ford is owned by Rod Whedbee of Rapid City, South Dakota. The graphics were applied by Billy "The Kid" Christine, using pink, blue, white, purple and green on the yellow background. Quite a change from the basic black that Henry Ford thought all cars should wear.*

Previous page

*Laying out scallops for painting is similar to the techniques used in laying out flames. And like flames, or any other style of custom painting for that matter, the design is limited only by your imagination and can be as wild or as mild as you like. Most scallop designs are symmetrical, so take care when transferring the shapes from one side of the car to the other. This yellow 1937 Ford Tudor from Texas uses the scallops to blend the two-tone paint scheme together, as the whole front end is painted in a light blue.*

*High-tech scallops in high-tech paint. Randy and Leslie High of Blue Springs, Missouri, chose for their ride a fenderless 1934 Chevrolet Roadster. The car is painted blue with the addition of the hot pink scallops. The removable top is also hot pink and the pink and blue theme is carried over into the engine compartment of this car. The details never end on this car: check out the front shock absorbers!*

80

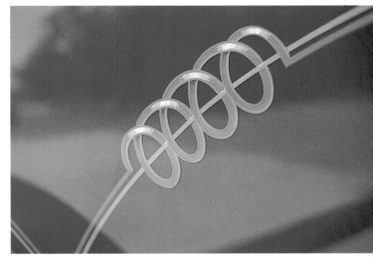

A comet-like swirl adds to the basic pinstriping work on this red rod. The spiral is painted pink, turquoise and dark blue using metallic particles in the paint.

More scallops, this time with color blended tips! Baby Blue has been under construction and owned by the Foss family of Montesano, Washington, since 1943. Some of the custom ideas may appear new but the most recently manufactured part dates back to 1957. Larry and Janice Foss have had the color baby blue on their car for several years now but the pink and purple scallops are a 1989 addition. The car was built to look like a 1950s car and the look works—with a bit of 1980s high-tech styling!

Next page

Modern graphics on old hot rods can work miracles. This 1933 Ford looks like an old-style track roadster of the 1930s and 1940s. Bill and Sharon Davis of Ortonville, Michigan, own the rod. Note the disc brake conversion for comfort and safety.

An artist at a labor of love. Billy "The Kid" Christine of Indianapolis, Indiana, is making his mark in the field of custom painting with the application of brushed-on graphics. His special touch is shown here being ap-

plied to the body of a yellow Model A Roadster owned by Rod Whedbee of Rapid City, South Dakota. Herb Martinez gives credit to Billy for teaching him this modern form of applying paint to customize cars.

Previous page

The high-tech graphics on this rod give new meaning to the phrase, "just a splash of color." This wild splash design creates a wave of interest wherever it goes. Mike Stubblefield of Pflugerville, Texas, is the driver and proud owner of this 1934 chopped Ford Tudor.

Opposite page

Jamus is a pinstriper of repute. Like most other professional pinstripers, he has a wide array of paints and brushes, although his favorite striping paint is Sign Painters One Shot. Here he dresses a 1957 Pontiac. Note his style of bracing his paint hand with his other fist. The addition of just a little paint in the proper place does wonders to the appearance of any car.

Name your paint style. Herb Martinez of San Francisco, California, has a sample board for you to see what the design will look like before it is actually painted on your car. Martinez travels to many shows each year and sets up shop to paint graphics or stripes on your car. In the past when graphics were sprayed on they had to be done in a shop; the modern graphics of the 1990s are being brushed on and the results are out of this world.

The custom painting on the vans in the early 1970s has played a big role in the custom painting of the 1980s and 1990s. Hand-painted murals, pictures and designs are still popular on the rods today. The vans had larger expanses of area to work with but this red pickup truck tailgate makes a fine palate for Tom Stratton of Tallahassee, Florida.

By the paint job on this car, you know it must be 1990 and not 1935. The top of this 1935 Ford is painted lime green and the bottom is painted black. The two colors are divided by yellow, blue and red graphics. The hood side panel is also customized; gone is the louvered side panel and in its place is a raised panel. The center of the wheels matches the top side's green.

Next page

At first glance this 1937 Ford Tudor appears to be painted two-tone. Take a closer look. It carries the Euro-look with everything painted from top to bottom: bumpers, door handles, mirrors, headlight rims—you name it! The only thing missing a splash of color is the wheels. The top of the car is magenta, the bottom is aqua. The division is marked by a pink graphic pinstripe. Overall, the appearance is clean and neat. The car is owned by Gary Stanifer of Whiteland, Indiana.